PRIVATE EYE

Colemanballs
12

A selection of quotes,
most of which originally appeared
in PRIVATE EYE's
'Colemanballs' column.

Our thanks once again to all the readers
who sent us their contributions,
and to whom this book is dedicated.

Dedicated to Larry
(1927 – 2003)

PRIVATE EYE

Colemanballs
12

Compiled and edited by
BARRY FANTONI

Illustrated by Tony Husband

PRIVATE EYE

Published in Great Britain
by Private Eye Productions Ltd,
6 Carlisle Street, London W1D 3BN

© 2004 Pressdram Ltd
ISBN 1 901784 36 3
Designed by Bridget Tisdall
Printed in Great Britain by
Cox and Wyman Ltd, Reading

Athletics

"It's a real shot in the foot for athletics."

JOHN RAWLING

"If there's a race between the slower man and the faster man there's only going to be one result."

JONATHAN DAVIES

"He's got his faith, his health and his family – but, more importantly, he's got a gold medal."

JAMIE THEAKSTON

"Olympic years are important because it's the Olympics."

RADIO 5 LIVE

"Two words that go together so well: Finnish distance running."

BRENDAN FOSTER

"It's gold or nothing... and it's nothing. He comes away with a silver medal."

DAVID COLEMAN

"Most of these athletes will have a favourite lead leg, which is either left or right."

MIKE WHITTINGHAM

"Is there something that sticks out that makes you an exceptional pole-vaulter?"

ADRIAN CHILES

"At this stage of the race being in front is a double-edged coin."

BBC2

"Jamie Quarry of Scotland lies in second place. Meanwhile, the leading Briton is in fifth place."

BBC NEWS 24

"The Commonwealth Games will be the biggest sporting event since September 11th."

CLASSIC FM NEWS

"That completes the heats of the 200 metres, as they say in the Eurovision Song Contest."

RUSSELL FULLER

"He looks behind him and sees that he only has one man in front of him."

BRENDAN FOSTER

"...that's an almost perfect false start."

BBC

"There will be 5000 competitors on the pitch, including, of course, the Queen..."

MIKE BUSHELL

Boxing

"The 25-year-old [Cory Spinks] is the son of former heavyweight champion Leon Spinks and former heavyweight title-holder Michael Spinks."

BBC SPORT WEBSITE

JONATHAN ROSS: It's good to see you still have all your marbles!
HENRY COOPER: Yeah, I boxed for 27 years, 11 as an amateur and 17 as a professional.

BBC RADIO 2

"I don't think anything was wrong tonight, it just went wrong."

BOXING OFFICIAL, BBC1

"Audley Harrison. He's 31 years old. He'll be 33 come the autumn."

JIM NEILLY

Cricket

"With regard to the broken finger, when batting I'll just have to play it by ear."

MARCUS TRESCOTHICK

"Greg Chappell instructed his brother Trevor to bowl the last ball underground…"

RICHARD KAUFMANN

"And you can't ignore what's going on under the water of the iceberg either."

CHRISTOPHER MARTIN JENKINS

"It's a very psychological sport, cricket – once the kingpin goes down, all the other puzzles just crumble away."

ANITA ANAND

"The Zimbabwean fans have been quite quiet; now there are dozens of them starting to expose themselves."

JONATHAN AGNEW

"We've had the main course and now it's time for the hors d'oeuvres and cheese."

DAVID LLOYD

"He's laid out his stall and is sticking to it."

HENRY BLOFELD

"Other than his mistakes, he hasn't put a foot wrong."

SIMON HUGHES

"It's a beautiful day today and as I look around the ground I can see about 30 young girls all wearing Dutch caps."

JONATHAN AGNEW

"He's taking the bull by the horns here, and throwing everything at it."

BOB WILLIS

"Clearly the West Indies are going to play their normal game, which is what they normally do."

TONY GRIEG

"That was a sort of parson's nose innings – good in parts."

CHARLES COLVILLE

"McCullum dispatched the bails to all four corners of the hemisphere."

RADIO SPORT NEW ZEALAND

"Pakistan always have the same problem – too many chiefs and not enough Indians."

ROBERT CROFT

"This shirt is unique, there are only 200 of them!"

RICHIE BENAUD

"England need to pick players who do not have skeletons in their coffins."

IAN BOTHAM

"It's only a matter of time before the end of this innings."

MICHAEL PESCHARDT

"Klusener holds that bat like a piece of wood..."

HENRY BLOFELD

"This game was another rung on the ladder of the learning curve."

JOHN EMBUREY

"The last rites are on the wall here."

ALLAN DONALD

"This morning he [Marcus Trescothick] has more or less left off where he carried on yesterday afternoon."

MICHAEL ATHERTON

"Their heads were on their chins..."

HENRY BLOFELD

Euroballs

"He [Zidane] goes into this if not the best player in the world, the best player in the world."

GARY LINEKER

"Sorry to interrupt myself..."

JOHN MOTSON

"Mentally, he's [John Terry] as strong as an ox."
MICHAEL OWEN

"Looks like he's got a bit of a knock there, judging by the language on his face."
CLIVE TYLDESLEY

"The overhead kick could have gone anywhere, but it didn't."

MARK BRIGHT

"Whether he [Wayne Rooney] will come as good as he has, only time will tell."

TREVOR BROOKING

"They've tasted the other side of the coin on so many occasions."

ANDY TOWNSEND

"Portugal had more possession but less of the ball..."

MARK LAWRENSON

"These tournaments come round every two years – we can't expect to win them every year."

MICHAEL OWEN

"With Zidane you expect the unexpected, but sometimes it just doesn't happen."

ITV

Football

"...and the Bulgarians are doing all they can here to waste every last inch of time in this game."
COLIN MACNAMARA

"His arms are down by his shoulders."
STAN COLLYMORE

"With the score at Scotland 6, Italy 7, Scotland are all at 6's and 7's."

GARY PARKER

"Roy Keane... didn't go through the book with a fine toothbrush."

TONY CASCARINO

"Matches don't come any bigger than FA Cup quarter-finals."

NEIL WARNOCK

"Football games turn on things that are done by players."

WILLIE MILLER

"... and he's fallen into a coma of competitiveness."

CLIVE TYLDESLEY

"Disbelieving Shrewsbury Town fans can't believe it."

RADIO SHROPSHIRE

"We lost to both cup winners last year, and you can't do more than that."

NEIL WARNOCK

"Our goalkeeper didn't have a save to make in 90 minutes. And yet he still ended up conceding four goals."

JOE ROYLE

"Oh dear, his right leg collided with himself there."

MARK BRIGHT

"I can't imagine we'd have had 60,000 at Old Trafford to watch Leichtenstein if the game had been played at Wembley."

RADIO 5 LIVE

"For Celtic, scoring three goals is like scoring twice as many as two in Europe."

DAVIE PROVAN

"Those Bradford fans with memories will be thinking back to last year..."

RAY FRENCH

"I've been asked that question for the last six months. It is not fair to expect me to make such a fast decision on something that has been put upon me like that."

TERRY VENABLES

"It's going to be difficult for me – I've never had to learn a language and now I do."

DAVID BECKHAM

"When I'm out on the pitch it's the closest thing to being back in a dressing room."

STEVE BAINES

"I bet Keegan will be jumping like a Jack in a Beanstalk."

SKY SPORTS NEWS

"Bristol City will be attacking their fans in the second half."

GEORGE GAVIN

"His body's not ready for the Premiership yet, let alone his body."

MARK LAWRENSON

"And the Premiership season is drawing to a conclusion on its first day..."

RAY STUBBS

"He [Martin O'Neill] was in a no-win situation, unless he won the match."

MURDO MACLEOD

"Newcastle can still make sure their hands are in their own destiny."

MARK SAGGERS

"The man [Alex Ferguson] is United. Cut him and he will bleed red..."

ALAN BRAZIL

"Today's been a good day for Wayne, but he's understood that on another day it could've been a bad day..."

DAVID MOYES

"Robbie Fowler has been scoring goals like that since before he was almost born."

KEVIN KEEGAN

"We had ten times as many shots on target as Bolton, and they had none at all..."

SIR BOBBY ROBSON

"Batistuta, 3 of 4 of his goals have come from the substitute's bench."

MARTIN TYLER

"Sometimes the underdog wins, sometimes the favourite doesn't."

SIR BOBBY ROBSON

"Champions League takes over centre stage from football tonight."

GARY RICHARDSON

"It was a great debut from Rooney. He's taken to it like a duck out of water."

GERRY FRANCIS

"Well, Clive, it's all about the two 'M's – movement and positioning."

RON ATKINSON

"You haven't not given up hope that you won't be in this division next year?"

MARK PUGACH

"I'm not going to pick out anyone in particular, but Jay Jay Okocha should not be the captain of a football club."

RODNEY MARSH

"We as a club and as a team don't hang our dirty washing out for other people."

PAT RICE

"Chelsea are the team who can break the Arsenal and Manchester United monopoly."

RON ATKINSON

"Referees don't come down here with a particular flavoured shirt on."

STEVE COPPELL

"Michael Owen is NOT a diver. He knows when to dive, and when not to..."

STEVE HODGE

"The under-20s... looking to maintain the magnificent Irish record in under-age football."

SKY SPORTS 1

"He turned on a sixpence like a thoroughbred horse."

GRAHAM SELLERS

"And the Liverpool goalkeeper Chris Kirkland has signed a contract which will keep him at the club until the start of the next century."

SIMON BROTHERTON

"You've taken the wind right out of my mouth."

RAY STUBBS

"They [Utd] seem to be in total, if not complete control."

JON CHAMPION

"They was given as good as they got."

JOHN TERRY

"We believe that the only way we can lose the game is if we lose it."

TONY CARROLL

"Neil Baker is standing on the touchline with hands in tracksuit bottoms scratching his head."

GRAHAM McGARRY

"He went down like a pack of cards."

CHRIS KAMARA

"He [Dennis Bergkamp] is like an English equivalent of Teddy Sheringham."

TREVOR BROOKING

"Last season was dark times for Swansea City but now with Lee Trundle they can see some light at the end of the rainbow."

IAN WALSH

"Rooney's got the world at his feet, if he can keep his feet on the ground."

GERRY FRANCIS

"We haven't had the rub of the dice."
                                    SIR BOBBY ROBSON

"The atmosphere here is thick and fast."
                                    CHRIS KAMARA

"Peter Beardsley... has got a few tricks up his book."
                                    IAN SNODIN

"The trouble with football these days is that there are too many Madonnas in the game."
                                    RADIO 5 LIVE

"Whatever happens, Scotland's squad will be concentrating on getting their second leg over successfully tonight."

BBC RADIO 4

"Macclesfield Town, with an opportunity to put the icing on the Christmas cracker..."

ADAM BRAZENDALE

"Whether Gordon Strachan is taking a sabbatical or will come back, we'll have to see."

BRYAN ROBSON

"He [Repka] has hardly been on the pitch as many times as he's played."

ALVIN MARTIN

"That's the sort of save he [David James] is capable of."

TREVOR BROOKING

"If we had taken our chances we would have won, at least."

DAVID O'LEARY

"He should have felt he probably scored then."

TREVOR BROOKING

"He's started anticipating what's going to happen before it's even happened."

GRAEME LE SAUX

"So, United then, all in red, with their white shorts and black socks."

FRASER DEIGNTON

"Liverpool – the only team in action in the Premiership. A good chance for them..."

DAMIEN JOHNSON

"Ameobi stretches out one of his long right legs..."

RADIO 5 LIVE

"...one team with destiny already decided..."

KEVIN KEEGAN

"The longer the game went on, you got the feeling that neither side really wanted to lose."

MARK LAWRENSON

"Sometimes, at the back of your head, you take your foot off the gasometer."

ALLY McCOIST

"I don't know if it's the first time twins have represented Wales, but it's certainly unique..."

RADIO WALES

"This is like pat-a-cake pat-a-cake butcher's man."

MARK LAWRENSON

"We need goals when the scoreline is 0-0."
SVEN GORAN ERIKSSON

"He [Steven Gerrard] wears his shirt on his sleeve..."

RADIO 5 LIVE

"Manchester United have scored at either end in this half."

RON ATKINSON

"Football's like a big market place, and people go to the market every day to buy their vegetables..."

SIR BOBBY ROBSON

"He needs to be brave now. And when I say 'brave' I mean 'brave' in the mental sense."

RON ATKINSON

"Wolves will be like lamb to the fodder tomorrow."

DAVE BEASANT

"We're at the top of a cliff and we can either fall off the edge or keep climbing."

GARY NEVILLE

"Gary Neville says that Porto are a bunch of girls who go down too easily."

PETER SCHMEICHEL

"Had we not got that second goal the score might well have been different."

DAVID PLEAT

"It is hard to imagine Crouch scoring his second had he not scored his first."

HYDER JAWAD

"Ian Pearce... has limped off with what looks like a shoulder injury."

TONY COTTEE

"Chris Kirkland... experienced shoulders on a young head."

RADIO 5 LIVE

"In the space of three second-half minutes Newcastle scored twice at the end of the first half."

JOHN MURRAY

"You felt this was the sort of game that needed a goal to break the deadlock."

RON JONES

"Pompey need to open Bolton's can of defensive thinking..."

SAM MATTAFACE

"Women are a large cross-section of society and that is a section of society we would very much like to penetrate."

MARK PALIOS

"In football, you can never say anything is certain. The benchmark is 38-40 points. That has always been the case. That will never change."

STEVE BRUCE

"He's not the sharpest sandwich in the picnic."
                                    TONY CASCARINO

"For nearly all the season we've been in the top half of the table and for most of the season better than that."

                                    ALAN CURBISHLEY

"If you can get through the first round you have a good chance of getting into the next one."

                                    NIGEL WORTHINGTON

"...1-0 is not a winning score, by any means..."
                                    IAN HALL

"He is the man who has been brought on to replace Pavel Nedved. The irreplaceable Pavel Nedved."

                                    CLIVE TYLDESLEY

"I was inbred into the game by my father."
                                    DAVID PLEAT

"Wayne Rooney really has a man's body on a teenager's head."

GEORGE GRAHAM

"It's his outstanding pace that stands out..."

ROBBIE EARLE

"Maine Road was a great football stadium but as time moved on it stayed where it is..."

KEVIN KEEGAN

"Chris Porter scored his first league goal last week, and he's done the same this week."

JEFF STELLING

"Del Piero, danger oozing from every vessel in his body..."

RADIO 5 LIVE

"Although we are playing Russian Roulette we are obviously playing Catch 22 at the moment and it's a difficult scenario to get my head round."

PAUL STURROCK

"He turned, and instinctively the ball was in the back of the net."

PAUL McDOWELL

"The players' breath is condensating as they come out of the tunnel."

DAVID CHILCOTT

"I can't fault Mark Palios too highly..."

JOHN MOTSON

"It's slightly alarming the way Manchester
United decapitated against Stuttgart."

MARK LAWRENSON

"He [Gerard Houlier] runs a very tightly knit
ship."

ROB HAWTHORNE

"Liverpool are currently halfway through an
unbeaten twelve-match run."

ALAN PARRY

"The final? If United and Arsenal get through the quarter-finals and can avoid themselves in the semis..."

MARK LAWRENSON

"There are more questions than answers being asked at the moment."

STAN COLLYMORE

"Thistle will need to score at least once if they want to win this game."

SANDY CLACK

"Yellow card for the dive, red card for the sending off..."

STEVE McCLAREN

"So, Trevor Brooking – 3-2 to Wolves. Where does the balance of this game lie now?"

JOHN MURRAY

"It was a last-minute end to the game, wasn't it?"

STEVE MAY

"He's one of the greatest players in the world, if not one of the greatest anywhere."

CHANNEL 4 NEWS

"How are they defensively, attacking-wise?"

RON ATKINSON

"I've always been a childhood fan of Liverpool."

HARRY KEWELL

"With eight or ten minutes to go, they were able to bring Nicky Butt back and give him fifteen to twenty minutes."

NIALL QUINN

"If you shut your eyes for a moment you wouldn't know it was a pre-season friendly."

MU TV

"... and now [Burnley] have got an extra yard of doubtness in their minds."

CHRIS KAMARA

"It's been a very long match now, in terms of the length of it."

ALISTAIR ALEXANDER

"What people have to remember about Hull City is that there are always eleven players playing against them."

TERRY DOLAN

"Ideally, we should be in second or third place in the league."

GERARD HOULIER

"A clash of heads there as the two players collided together, at the same time."

CHRIS KAMARA

"Come on, Bury fans – you've got your night in the sun."

ADRIAN CHILES

"I've watched Tottenham for 20 years and never seen them decapitate like that before."

TALK SPORT

"Obviously it would be tough playing up in the Premiership next season, but I wouldn't lose any sleepless nights."

ALAN PARDEW

"They've taken the horns by the scruff of the neck."

TONY CASCARINO

"There's no doubt we'll be seen as a big fish in the First Division next year – everybody will be trying to knock us off our perch..."

KEVIN BLACKWELL

"United will be quite happy if they only lose by two or a couple of goals..."

RON ATKINSON

"Ronaldo hardly had a kick – until he got a head to Figo's cross."

GUY MOWBRAY

"He [Milner] seems to be holding his shoulder, in the shoulder area."

GRAHAM TAYLOR

"Football is much harder if you don't have the ball."

SVEN GORAN ERIKSSON

"He [Henrik Larson] was on the six-yard line, just two yards away from the goal."

PAT NEVIN

"We owe it to ourselves first and foremost, and, more importantly, to our fans."

KEVIN KEEGAN

Golf

"If someone had offered me a 69 this morning,
I'd probably have taken it."

RICHARD JOHNSON

Horses

"He has broken his left leg, which is a real kick in the teeth for him."

LUKE HARVEY

"Nice little horse... gelded him... made a man out of him."

BRYAN SMART

Literally

"The police were literally swimming in a sea of red herrings..."

BBC

"He literally looked like a fish out of water."

WILLIE THORNE

"We are talking about families literally dissolving in a sea of alcohol."

LORD ADEBOWALE

"In Athletics, the triple jumpers are literally the human kangaroos."

BBC

"A lot of these riders literally exploding on the mountain..."

PAUL SHERWIN

"He literally threaded the ball through the eye of a needle."

BBC RADIO SCOTLAND

"Derby County's chickens have literally come home to roost this season."

COLIN GIBSON

"Terry Venables has literally had his legs cut off from underneath him three times while he's been manager."

BARRY VENISON

"Elderly people can literally go downhill quite rapidly."

RADIO 5 LIVE

"It is hard to keep your feet on the ground when you are flying to literally the four corners of the globe."

GORDON LORENZ

"...riding a typical McCoy race where, with five lengths to go, he literally picks up the horse and carries it over the line."

CLARE BALDING

"Literally every second of every day, we are all growing a minute older..."

CORIN SWEET

"Derby County's previous directors had literally been burying their heads in the sand for years."

COLIN GIBSON

Motor Sport

"It was just like a plane crash – cars everywhere!"

JAMES COURTNEY

"...and Michael Schumacher just stood on his seat and pulled out something special."

MARTIN BRUNDELL

"That's another nail in his afternoon."

MARK BLUNDELL

Music

"We don't do things by halves on this show. Here is the third movement of Bach's Brandenburg Concerto No. 4."

LISA DUNCOMBE

"This is the tenth year of the show, that's ten decades of music."

JOOLS HOLLAND

"We're about to splice the mainbrace on Classic FM because we're going sailing with Katchaturian and Spartacus."

CLASSIC FM

"Coming next – the music you'd like to hear at your funeral."

ANDY ARCHER

"He [William Lloyd-Webber] died without telling anyone."

SIMON BATES

Oddballs

"Me and the children are flying backwards all the time."

VICTORIA BECKHAM

"I just wanted to steal something as a momentum."

DENISE VAN OUTEN

"Every second of every day, we're all getting a minute older..."

RADIO SCOTLAND

"Ninety-five per cent of children are murdered by their parents..."

GRAYSON PERRY

"The freezing conditions are making it difficult driving underfoot."

RADIO LEEDS

"And she rises from the water like a sphincter."

CRAIG CHARLES

"It's a floating city, there's absolutely no other word for it – it's a floating hotel."

MIKE PARRY

"Is that down to public apathy or do you think people just don't care anymore?"

ANNIE OTHEN

"What are the pitfalls of getting close to a serial killer?"

JENNY MURRAY

"I've never met a single woman who's happy with the way she looks, except Jordan, although I've never met her."

RICHARD MADELEY

"The twins, who are joined at the head, both come from Egypt."

BBC RADIO 1

"The Washington gunman has demanded a ransom of $10m – his motive is unknown."

READING 107FM

"Sir Isaac Newton pretty much invented gravity."

TOM PARKS

"Jeremy Beadle becomes an MBE for his charitable services. He is said to have raised around £10m for charities in as many years."

BBC CEEFAX

"Once he'd died, his life was over."

LULU

"We are not prepared to let one rotten apple in the barrel take the reputation of the Scottish pig industry..."

BBC

"Afterwards we were told that the cameras trained on us as we sat on the toilets were fake. I was so relieved."

MARLI BUCK

"Viagra manufacturer Pfizer is facing stiff competition from rival pharmaceutical firms."

LONDON NEWSTALK RADIO

"I still go back to the Old Testament and read Revelations."

DAVID BOWIE

"I don't think we should all be starving in our garrisons."

TRACEY EMIN

"Messner was a great mountaineer, but now he's 59. Surely he's past his peak?"

BILL WHITEFORD

"When I was Bishop of London I had a large number of gay clergy."

JIM THOMPSON

"They do not come any bigger than Bank of America, the third largest bank."

JOHN TERRETT

"Some couples are so famous that they're recognisable from just their first names – Posh and Becks."

RADIO 4

"This is the first time since her death that the Queen Mother hasn't been here."

LOOK EAST

"...and if millions and millions of us are wearing M&S underwear, why are they falling down?"

CHRISTINE HAMILTON

"Nobody in their right minds would want to be in a psychiatric hospital."

DR MIKE HARRIS

"The vendetta is on the other foot."

SIR CHRISTOPHER BLAND

"He looks a bit like Jacques Cousteau, and he certainly does know the secrets of the deep when it comes to tyre technology."

JAMES ALLEN

"Halle Berry had a lovely pair of teeth."
EAMONN HOLMES

"You could earn £50k a year as a plumber, but you could break your leg and then you would have nothing to fall back on."

RADIO 4

"Initial reports suggest that between one and two people have been killed."

BBC

"To speak to a travel adviser, press 2.
Otherwise your call will be transferred to a
travel adviser."

LONDON TRAVEL INFORMATION LINE

"Sleeping with David Beckham was a
momentous day for me, not just a one-night
stand..."

SARAH MARBECK

"As yet there has been no reaction from the man
who was murdered."

BBC NEWS 24

"He [Michael Jackson] is a child trapped in the body of a five-year-old man."

URI GELLER

"The former Archbishop resigned following criticism of his handling of a convicted paedophile priest."

RADIO 4

"If blood is thicker than water, it must also be thicker than a calendar or a small clock."

ESTHER RANTZEN

"Time stood still for a couple of seconds then."

SKY SPORTS

"I think that longevity and long-lived success is something that most artists would die for..."

BEN BRADSHAW

"Her death marked a breakthrough which has yet to change the world in ways that we don't know."

PALAB GHOSH

"James Joyce wrote Ulysses in Paris, as did
Samuel Beckett."

EDNA O'BRIEN

"Where were you first born?"

JOOLS HOLLAND

"There was a sense of anticipation – at least
beforehand!"

GUY RUDDLE

"By 2012, a third of every adult will be obese."
DR HILLARY JONES

"If you play with fire, you're gonna get stung."

NASN

"The gap between the two men appears to be insurmountable."

TIM EWART

"People need to be taught how to put a condom on… these are things that have to be taught and they have to be rammed home quite hard…"

FI GLOVER

"We want to go upwards, not stand still and go backwards..."

CHRIS ROBINSON

"It's old... older than when Jonah was in the Ark."

SIMON BATES

"The problem is dead in the water unless something is pulled out of the fire."

BRIAN ROWAN

"All in all, a good year for female actresses..."

LBC

"The television watchdog upheld 69 complaints about the use of sexual innuendo in the Carling Black Label advert."

BBC ONLINE

"The vast majority of HIV sufferers will bend over backwards to ensure the safety of their partners."

COLIN DICKSON

"He seems to be taking his time, but his brain must be going ten to the dozen."

HAZEL IRVINE

"More than 30 percent of Americans are obese – and that figure is expanding."

DISCOVERY CHANNEL WEBSITE

"I've been a parent longer than I've been alive."

TOM HANKS

"They thought they had a golden goose they wanted to fleece."

PETER PARCHER

"Like everybody else, I've got four children..."
DAVE STEWART

"Going through that crowd is a once-in-a-lifetime experience. I did it once on the way out and once on the way in."

JON TICKLE

"Reverend John, who is living with an openly gay partner, is no doubt feeling rather sore today."

PAUL HANDLEY

"Zoos provide a very useful breeding ground for extinct species."

LOWRY TURNER

"I didn't see the point of hiding a bushel under a carpet..."

MEL B.

"Of course it's not against the law to bring children into this country illegally..."

VICTORIA DERBYSHIRE

"The sea quickly ebbed in…"

FIONA FOSTER

"You should not leave someone's ashes on a doorstep, whether they are deceased or not."

TOM BULL (FUNERAL SERVICES DIRECTOR)

"Our raison d'etre is to perform in English…"

PAUL DANIELS

"Some of our customers find it very daunting coming to a weight loss advisory meeting. For some of them, it's difficult even to get through the door."

WEIGHTWATCHERS SPOKESMAN

"The Daily Mail... Here's a story about Princess Diana's mother who didn't speak to her daughter for four months after her death."

BILL TURNBILL

"That's just a footnote at the back of my head."

VAL JOYCE

"People are bending over backwards to protect their own backs."

JOHN GREENWAY

"Fennel has a fennel flavour."

GARY RHODES

"If anyone keeps doing it [hiding], they'll be out of the door quicker than what they walked into it."

DAVE JONES

"Animal rights activists today welcomed the decision by Cambridge University not to build a centre for medical research, using monkeys."

RADIO 4

"It's the homosexual kiss in the middle of the film that has really got tongues wagging."

RACHEL HARVEY

"Let's not put the willies up a lot of people who are having IVF."

SHARON ALLCOCK

"Breaking news... I'm just hearing about the death of the actor, wit and raconteur Peter Ustinov... a living legend...."

MATTHEW WRIGHT

"He's hanging on by the thread of his fingertips."

JAY ROACH

"That sniper story... some bullet points..."

MIKE PARRY

"I have sown a few seeds and thrown a few hand grenades and I am now waiting for the dust to settle so that I can see how all the jigsaw bits come together."

GARY JOHNSON

Politics

"Conservatives must win the next election – not for ourselves, but for the hard-working, law-abiding people of Britain."

IAIN DUNCAN SMITH

"We are going big guns with humanitarian aid in southern Iraq."

BBC

"Barry Legg had a foot in all three camps."

ANDREW HOSKIN

"You could call it a complicated game of bluff.
Except that it's not a game. And they're not
bluffing."

ANDREW MARR

"The Hutton Enquiry has knocked Iraq off the
front pages."

KIRSTY YOUNG

"Israel's population has grown by over 20% in
the last ten years. Meanwhile, the Palestinian
population is exploding."

ALAN JOHNSTONE

"The government is ruining all the public services, particularly health, education and crime…"

IAIN DUNCAN SMITH

"Gordon Brown has a huge headache on his hands."

ADAM BOULTON

"It keeps that pot boiling, and he [Tony Blair] needs that boil to be lanced."

TIM MARSHALL

"I'm now in my 70th decade…"

THERESA GORMAN

"Iraqis are sick of foreign people coming in their country and trying to destabilise their country, and we will help them rid Iraq of these killers."

GEORGE W. BUSH

"An invisible hand stepped in and stopped the agreement."

BILL MORRIS

"We seem to be dancing to the wrong agenda."

KEITH VAZ

"Gordon Brown is not a man to hide his hat under a bushel."

RADIO SCOTLAND

"People should be reminded that America's reason for going to war was weapons of mass destruction. So far, all they've found is a tiny bit of botox."

STOP THE WAR COALITION SPOKESMAN

"This is one red herring that is going to sink in discussion."

DENIS McSHANE

"We have no plans for pauses or ceasefires or anything else."

DONALD RUMSFELD

"Building houses for affordable people..."

JOHN PRESCOTT

"I support Michael Howard for the leadership. He's highly articulous..."

CONSERVATIVE VOTER

"The terrorist attacks threaten to derail the road-map before it's got off the ground."

NEWSREADER

"You can say the decision was wrong, but I suspect if I'd been making the same decision then I would probably have made the same decision."

JOHN PRESCOTT

"The people of Northern Ireland should step back and ask themselves have they moved on..."

TONY BLAIR

Question & Answer

ROB MCLEAN: John Hartson is playing superbly today.
SANDY CLARK: Yes, Rob, there's no one better today.
ROB MCLEAN: So, Sandy, who is your man of the match?
SANDY CLARK: Alan Thompson.

BBC SCOTLAND

INTERVIEWER: What has separated
the sides [Manchester United and Tottenham]?
RON ATKINSON: Not much... United have
done most of the running, and they've almost
forced the big issue on them.

ITV

RAY STUBBS: That's [Manchester Utd 0
Fulham 1] a great start for Fulham, Mark.
MARK LAWRENSON: Yes, and paradoxically
it's a terrible start for United.

RADIO 5 LIVE

BRIAN HAMILTON: I think in the end it will
be down to Manchester United and Arsenal.
VICTORIA DERBYSHIRE: So you clearly
haven't ruled out Liverpool then?

RADIO 5 LIVE

PRESENTER: So describe your body position when a ball is released.
MIKE ATHERTON: Knees bent, with my head directly between my feet.

CHANNEL 4

ADRIAN CHILES: So who's Richmond playing today?
RICHMOND COACH: Jersey.
ADRIAN CHILES: Where are they from?
RICHMOND COACH: Jersey.

BBC

MATTHEW BANNISTER: Were you rooting for Celtic?
GUEST MP: No, but that's not because I wasn't rooting for Celtic.

RADIO 5 LIVE

RICHARD MADELY: So what are you going to spend your winnings on?
CONTESTANT: A wheelchair.
RICHARD: Oh why, what's the problem?
CONTESTANT: I'm disabled.
RICHARD: Great.

CHANNEL FOUR

SIMON BATES: You're off to Moscow, you and your husband... Have you ever been before?
COMPETITION WINNER: Well, I went when I was at school.
SIMON BATES: So you've never been before...

CLASSIC FM

Rugby

"They'll try to kick it into touch, as it's the only way to keep the ball in play."

BBC

"I'm disappointed to get a five weeks [after kneeing Duncan McRae of Saracens] but there will be no knee-jerk reaction."

MARTIN JOHNSON

"If we win, we'll go further in the competition...
that's the carrot dangling down the track."

MATT WILLIAMS

"The Irish lock forward Malcolm O'Kelly
playing his socks off his back..."

JIM NEILLY

"He's been sent to the Sin Bin... so they'll miss
his absence for the next 10 minutes..."

RUGBY SPECIAL

"We [Saracens] have all the ingredients for a
good mayonnaise; all we need is the stove at the
right temperature."

THOMAS CASTAIGNEDE

Snooker

"I know people say that Ronnie O'Sullivan is the best thing in snooker since Tiger Woods..."

WILLIE THORNE

"It's what you dream about when you are a kid, playing in the big games, and it doesn't come any bigger than the semi final."

RONNIE O'SULLIVAN

"Well he's conceded there, but he never gives up, does he Steve?"

JOHN PARROTT

"He [Jimmy White] has popped out to the toilet to compose himself before the final push."

STEVE DAVIS

"This is one of those matches where you feel neither player wants to lose."

JOHN VIRGO

"This looks like being the longest frame in the match, even though it's the first."

CLIVE EVERTON

"All the reds are in the open now, apart from the blue."

JOHN VIRGO

"When I was 5-1 down I thought I was going to lose 18-0."

RONNIE O'SULLIVAN

"If you take your foot off the pedal and treat thc game with contempt, then the balls have a habit of jumping up and kicking you in the teeth."

JOHN VIRGO

"It's two immovable objects clashing together..."

STEVE DAVIS

"Mark is facing defeat in the face."

JOHN VIRGO

"I'll never set foot on a snooker table again..."

MARK KING

"Nothing less might not be good enough."

JOHN VIRGO

Swimming

"We are hoping that our swimmers are going to do something big in the pool."

DIANE MODAHL

"England could not have had a better start – a silver medal for Tony Ally in the diving."

CHANNEL 4 NEWS

"The backstroke needs a lot of stamina at the beginning and middle of the race... and of course at the end."

ADRIAN MOREHOUSE

Tennis

"She [Serena Williams] played some great shots, but so did I, and that was the only difference."

JENNIFER CAPRIATI

"It's always been mandatory. We've never insisted the players do it."

MR GORRINGE

"I'm not worried about the weekend, I'm worried about Saturday."

PETE SAMPRAS

"Let's hope his nerves will run through his veins."

JOHN McENROE

"Anytime you're playing sport at this level, it's about winning or losing."

TIM HENMAN

"Tim's got a big job to do, so he's got to get out there and do his business."

VIRGINIA WADE

"Henman's injured shoulder has raised its ugly head again"

JONATHAN OVEREND

"The shoulder has made some big strides over the last 10 days to two weeks."

BBC NEWS WEBSITE

"Henman has made the semi-finals for four of the last five years so his Wimbledon record is second to none."

JEREMY BATES

"This poor guy's gonna walk out of here on a stretcher."

JOHN McENROE

"It's disappointing to have lost – that's the bee's knees of it..."

TIM HENMAN

"Henman should leave here with his head hung high..."

JONATHAN OVEREND

"For ten years Schalken has been in the world's top fifty or better..."

BBC

"It was a good shot, but he didn't execute it very well."

ANNABEL CROFT

"He [Andy Roddick] doesn't make mistakes, only when he has to."

ANDREW CASTLE

Wrestling

"That was a high-risk manoeuvre because the risk was high."

TAZ

Yachting

"Valencia will be hosting the next America's Cup – this is because Switzerland, who won it last time, has no sea round its coastline."

TIM DURRANT